Sayings
on the
Riches of Life

collected by
Rosemary May Wells

Books by Rosemary May Wells

God is an Onion
Wells of Thought

With grateful thanks to Sue Wheeler for the cover image
and to Annie Dickson for help with editing.

For Quakers

*who recognise the value of brief thought to illuminate life
and to whom I owe so much*

Contents

Introduction

I have always had an eclectic mind and enjoyed collecting quotes, especially of a philosophical, faith kind. The question at the back of my mind has always been:

How does faith relate to life?

So over the years I have jotted down quotes from all kinds of sources that spoke to me. Maybe they were simply thought-provoking. For some I was surprised at the author. Humorous ones express a certain light-heartedness running through life. Others I felt neatly encapsulated an answer folk may be looking for, like: You haven't lost faith, only lost sight of faith. Together they illustrate the puzzle of life.

Belonging to two traditions, both Church and the Religious Society of Friends or Quakers, has fed my inner life from two different angles, one the certainty of faith, the other more the questioning. So included are pieces of ministry offered over many years from the Quaker Meeting for Worship to which I belong, and some thoughts tossed off over coffee morning chat...It will introduce those unfamiliar with Quaker worship to the freedom of thought, and also the questioning, that those who seek but cannot accept conventional answers may express.

These I have marked with a **Q**.

Above all, I hope these sayings may give understanding and insight into life within the context of faith in the love of God underpinning all life.

Rosemary Wells
December 2020

My Life

Quakers say that 'letting your life speak' matters more than formal belief.
These quotes indicate the importance of our individual lives although they
cannot be fully realised apart from relationship to another or a group.

I want to shout the Gospel with my life.
  Charles de Foucould

I must become we before I can grow.
  Carl Jung

Glory be to God in heaven, glory be to God in me.
  A Russian acclamation

You have lived what others are praying for.(**Q**)

You need a place where you can belong,
yet feel you can still be yourself. (**Q**)

I am a single drop.
How can it be
That the whole ocean, God,
Flows into me.
  Angelus Silesius. 1624–1677

We may feel on the edge, yet know we are essential at the centre. (**Q**)

Life is ours to be spent not saved.

I read in a book that a man called Christ
went about doing good. It is very disconcerting
that I am so satisfied with just going about.
  Kagawa (Japanese Christian)

Be your own palace or the world's a jail.
Anon

Even a slug is a star if it dares to be its horned and slimy self.
John Hargrave

I am a new person who is you and me together.
T.S.Eliot

You were once wild here. Don't let them tame you.
Isadora Duncan

In the depths of winter, I finally learnt
that within me lay an invincible summer.
Albert Camus

Let life live you.
Tao of Pooh

I do life. I don't just talk about it. (**Q**)

In Elizabethan times you did your life.
It wasn't something done to you.

You recognise those on the same wave length because life speaks to life.

We only value each other as mortals
when we treat each other as immortals.
A man's main task in life is to give birth to himself.
Erich Fromm

I am a stranger and afraid
In a world I never made.
Stevie Smith

Accept the impotence of your humanity.
   Michael Tippett in A Child of our Time

Life lessons

We learn much through life experience but do we remember to remember what we learn and apply it ? As life experience accumulates we gain a changing perspective. Here is a ragbag selection of thoughts that interested me.

The best things in life just happen.
   Hugo Gryn – Chief Rabbi

If we have treats all the time,
   then nothing is special.

Life is to be lived out; it is not a problem to be solved.

Everyone has some question they don't want asked.

Expecting life to treat you well because you are a good person is like expecting an angry bull not to charge because you are a vegetarian.
   Shari R Barr

Against stupidity even the gods struggle in vain.
   Ancient wisdom

The sensible become foolish and the foolish become wise.

Correction does much; encouragement does more.
   Goethe

Answers are never easy and not always necessary.
To be able to live with questions is a great freedom –
the real question in any situation is: What is loving? (Q)

Life is not here to be regretted but to be lived.

I thought I'd worked out all the answers
when they changed the questions.

It is better to learn early of the inevitable depths, for then sorrow
and death take their proper place in life, and one is not afraid.
   Pearl Buck

Life is like a grindstone – whether it grinds you down
or polishes you up is up to your character.

If we all pulled in one direction the world would topple over.
   Yiddish Proverb

Life can only be understood backwards; but it must be lived forwards.
   Soren Kierkgaard

A mother said of her teenage son: I don't mind what he does for a job.
'If he takes a mundane job it gives him time and energy to pursue his
interests. If he's stretched to capacity in his work all he wants to do in
his spare time is recover. (Q)

The qualities that make a child attractive
are not necessarily appreciated in the man.

Why does life have to be so confusing ? I don't want to grow up.
   The cry of a 9 year old child

Maybe in any age it will always be the few who have the courage to
stand out from the crowd and against the injustices of society, risk
their all for Christ, their lives for a cause.

You may get to the very top of the ladder
and then find it has not been leaning against the right wall.
   A. Raine

A 16 year old boy was asked to clean the windows and polish the silver in lieu of a more interesting job. When grandma apologised for this dull job, he responded: I like polishing silver, seeing it come up brightly, and while I do it my mind floats free.

We can all make more of what we have
if we don't see ourselves as victims. (Q)

Laughter

Humour, wit, laughter – the sanity of life. Without it we would all go mad. To have a good belly-laugh does us all good.

Laughter is the joyous, universal evergreen of life.
  Abraham Lincoln

God needs a good laugh.
It's the only thing that keeps him going.
  (Q in conversation)

Do not worry about temptation.
As you get older it starts avoiding you.
  Anon

Laughter is the most civilised sound.
  Peter Ustinov

We are going to have peace if we have to fight for it.
  Dwight Eisenhower

Lord, fill my mouth with worthwhile stuff
and shut it when I've said enough.

He does not know his God who is afraid to laugh with him.
  George McDonald – poet and pastor

That which is called firmness in a king
is called obstinacy in a donkey.
  John Erskine

When sorrow is sacred, humour is in doubt.
  Robert Bridges – Testament of Beauty

If we all work together, we can totally disrupt the system.
Anon

The only reason why some people get lost in thought
is because it is unfamiliar territory.
Paul Fix

I like getting into hot water. It keeps me clean.
G. K. Chesterton

Kindness

Kindness is an underrated quality. It lifts the burden of life and here I have included satellite qualities like gentleness and understanding.

Kindness is a language that the deaf can hear
and the blind can read.
  Mark Twain

The fulness of truth will be like God's knowledge of us –
not harsh but understanding.
  Richard Harries

Yet in my Walks it seems to me that the Grace of God is in Courtesy
  Hilaire Belloc

There is nothing stronger in the world than gentleness.
  Han Suyin

The finest quality you can find in your fellowman is kindness.
  Rupert Brooke

Civilisation is made up of millions of unregarded
acts of kindness.
  George Elliott

Why can't people give others a piece of their heart
rather than a piece of their mind.
  Des Marshall

People will forget what you said, people will forget what you did,
but people will never forget how you made them feel.
  Viki Williams

The longest journey in life is from the mind to the heart.

That best portion of a good man's life,
His little, nameless, unremembered, acts of Kindness and of love.
  William Wordsworth

Friendship

Friendship is the only relationship that holds by its own inner dynamism without any external guarantee or commitment.

A child to a grownup teaching helper:
You are my friend. Look after yourself. (**Q**)

Sow the seeds of friendship
As your way you wend,
And you reap a blessing
At the journey's end.
  Anon

Some friendships do not last,
but some friends are more loyal than brothers.
  Proverbs 18: 24

It is a good thing to be rich,
It is a good thing to be strong,
But it is a better thing
To be loved by many people.

Don't walk before me,
I may not follow.
Don't walk behind me,
I may not lead.
Walk beside me
and be my friend.
  Albert Camus

Friendship is to people what sunshine is to flowers.

We're given our family, thank God, we choose our friends.

Abraham was called the friend of God.
James 2: 23

From quiet homes and first beginnings,
Out to the undiscovered ends,
There's nothing worth the wear of winning
But laughter and the love of friends.
Hilaire Belloc

Happiness

The purpose of life is to be happy' – and why not ? Most of us wouldn't think to be miserable the purpose of life. But how to be happy, that is not so obvious. Here are a few hints.

I shall always work to advance the happiness
and prosperity of my peoples.
   Queen Elizabeth 11. – 8th February 1952

To watch the corn grow, and the blossom set;
to draw hard breath over ploughshare or spade;
to read, to think , to love, to hope, to pray –
these are the things that make us happy.
   John Ruskin

It takes courage to be happy.

It is better to be happy than right.

All the animals except man know that
the principle business of life is to enjoy it.
   Samuel Butler

When in unexpected moments,
I feel blessed by a sense of contentment
I catch a thread, a glimpse
Of this mystery that waits for me
Like a patient guest.
   Anon

Wherever a cat sits,
there shall happiness be found.
   Stanley Spencer

Contentment lies in organising the self
in the direction of simplicity.
  Hebridean Altars

Sorrow that has no vent in tears makes other organs weep.
  Henry Maudsley

Why is the sheer pleasure
of a healthy bowel-movement unmentionable ?
  Anon

Be happy. Keep the faith. Do little things. (**Q**)

The greatest pleasure I know is to do a good action
by stealth and to have it found out by accident.
  Charles Lamb

Honeymoon – the first month after marriage when
there is nothing but tenderness and pleasure
  Samuel Johnson's dictionary

St Augustine said the purpose of preaching was
to teach, to give delight, to move.

You do not know your own blessedness.
  Robert Louis Stevenson

She is happy, content. She does not expect too much of life.
  In conversation

Happiness is the art of making a bouquet of the flowers within reach.

Time

Time is elusive. It can disappear or seem to stretch for ever. It connects the past, the ancient past, the present and the future. It can also mean opportunity – we must grasp the moment.

The real problem of humanity is the following:
we have palaeolithic emotions, medieval institutions, and godlike technology.
  Edward O Wilson

We commend the past to your healing, the present to your care and the future to your providence.

When the time is right the way will open.

In times of profound change, the learners inherit the earth, while the learned find themselves beautifully equipped to deal with a world that no longer exists.
  Eric Hoffer

Some people always have a feeling of unfulfilledness – maybe there is more in the personality than can be fulfilled in one life-time.
  Jean Vanier

Everything has its time:
The Lord of time is God.
The turning point of time is Christ.
The right spirit of the times is the Holy Spirit.
  Karl von Hase – grandfather of Dietrich Bonhoeffer

I can't afford to waste my time making money. (Q)

About a Quaker who joined the Society at 93 :
'She's a slow learner.'

Love, support, time. –
the greatest thing a parent can give a child. (Q)

When Nelson Mandela was out of prison he was asked:
'Are you not bitter at the way you were treated ?'
He responded: 'Of course I'm bitter, but there's work to be done. One
cannot spend time in bitterness.'

It is a mistake to think too much about the future.
Only one link in the chain of destiny can be handled at a time.
   Winston Churchill

Time, you old gypsy man,
Will you not stay,
Put up your caravan
Just for one day ?
   Ralph Hodgson

Time flies
Suns rise and fall
Let time go by
Love is forever over all.
   On an old sundial.

Imagination

Many people are full of good will but I sometimes wonder if we don't lack the imagination to go with it. Here are thoughts about and examples of the imagination.

Does love make you think ? It certainly does.
Without love you're dull. (Q)

Birds are God's poetry on life.
  Anon

Imagination is more important than knowledge.
  Einstein

Solitude is as needful to the imagination
as society is wholesome for the character.
  James Russell Lowell. 1819–1891

One insight is worth a life-time's experience.

Imagination is the way in to prayer.(Q)

You do not know another man until
you have walked a mile in his moccasins.
  Indian Proverb

A dry cleaners had a notice on the door:
If you are unemployed and going for a job interview,
we will clean your suit for you, free of charge.

What a wonderful sweep of the imagination it was when poets first
called the humblest flower the daisy, which is the Day's eye, thus

shedding the perennial light of the world
upon the small and passing joys of life.
Howard Spring

Imagination is the friend of possibility.
John O'Donohue

I dwell in possibility. A fairer house than prose.
Emily Dickinson

Leisure

For years I have had the feeling that the world is like a spinning top, spinning faster and faster, and leisure gets squeezed out by activity. Some of these thoughts suggest that it has always been a tendency in human life.

this strange disease of modern life
with its sick hurry, its divided aims,
its heads o'er taxed, its palsied hearts.
  Matthew Arnold – The Scholar Gypsy. 1853

It is in our idleness, in our dreams,
that the submerged truth sometimes rises to the top.
  Virginia Woolf

50 years after climbing Mt Everest:
"We did not think we had conquered Everest.
We felt the mountain had relented."
  Sir Edmund Hilary

Maybe withdrawing is nature's way of protecting one's sanity.
  Christina Noble

The family that plays together, stays together.

However poor, it is important to remember that
self-indulgence is one of the great pleasures of life.
  Anon

Work is not always required of a man.
There is such a thing as sacred idleness, the cultivation
of which is now fearfully neglected.
  George MacDonald. (1824–1905)

Worship, work, study and play –
the mantra of the Othona Community

Music and Art

Music, art, the whole range of culture is what gives many people meaning in life. It is not accidental that all religions have expressed themselves through creative beauty.

My art is to be found in every English hedgerow
and in every English lane.
  John Constable

Not without design does God write the music of our lives.
  John Ruskin

Darwin in old age:
I wish I'd spent more time reading poetry.

Music – the gate that separates the earthly from the heavenly.
  Hugh McDiarmid

Only two things lift one above the misery of life: music and cats.
  Dr. Schweitzer

Without music, life would be an error.
  Nietzsche

He who plays the piano stays sane.
  Italian saying

I love all beauteous things
I seek and adore them.
God has no better praise,
And man in his hasty days
Is honoured for them.
  Robert Bridges

After the bread queue massacre in Sarajevo a cellist went there every
Saturday morning and played Albinoni's Adagio.

Everything has its beauty but not everyone sees it.
Confucian

Words

I have always loved words but felt because of their power they need to be used carefully. Language is essential but it can make or mar communication.

The business of the novelist is to show the sorry-ness
underlying the grandeur of things
and the grandeur underlying the sorriest of things.
   Thomas Huxley

The man who does not read good books has no
advantage over the man who can't read them.
   Mark Twain

There is no friend as loyal as a book.
   Ernest Hemingway

I have a great capacity for accepting the religious language of other
people although it may not be the language I would use myself. (**Q**)

Lord, fill my mouth with worthwhile stuff –
and shut it when I've said enough.

The chief glory of a nation is its authors.
   (quoted by Carnegie)

Thoughts are your own; words are so no longer.
   Anon

Perspective and Influence

The people who influence us most in life may change our perspective.
They help us to see life from a different angle and so give us the courage to
change. Often they are totally unaware of this – wouldn't they be sur-
prised to know !

You have raised us from the ordinary to the special. (**Q**)

I so feel for those who try. (**Q**)

History gives a sense of belonging.
A young assistant at Dorchester museum

We are all self-centred until we have children.
Then we realise we are part of a wider whole.
Anon

Celebrity culture makes others feel a failure.

Nobody is indispensable but some are irreplaceable.
Anon

Outsiders have an insight that insiders may miss.
Anon

You never know when someone may be touched
by the eternal.
R4 Service of Worship

We come to Meeting not only to fuel the lamps,
but to clean the glass so that others may see the light. (**Q**)

The Good Samaritan answered the immediate need.
He didn' start a cause to clear up crime on the Jericho road. (Q)

In the end it is consistency you want in people, not perfection. Betrayal is to find them do what you would not have expected. Just that.
    Penelope Lively

Youth and Age

Growing up, maturing through life's experiences, we may have mixed feelings but I hope these thoughts suggest that older age has something special to give as well as youth.

The day the child realises that all adults are imperfect he becomes adolescent. The day he forgives them he becomes adult. The day he forgives himself he becomes wise.

Anon

Why does life have to be so complicated.
I don't want to have to grow up.

9 year old girl

Discipline – that's their security in the future.
Discipline guarantees security.

Mother, re her children

To children who are given too much
you deny the capacity for experiencing great joy.

Mavis Klein

Older people need appreciation more as their
powers fail; they need to know they can still give. (Q)

I'd like to live a few more years. The world is so interesting,
I want to know what happens (Q)

As a young man as a war correspondent you imagine
you are helping to change the world.
As an older man, you realise you've done nothing to
change it, you have only shown how it's been.

A war correspondent

When you are young you live life.
When you are older you savour life.
Anon

I so enjoyed being young. I would give up all the security and the experience of maturity – they say you gain – for being young again. (**Q**)

Maturity consists in blessing our origins.

Risk and Protection

Life is a risk and we all hope for protection. We protect our children and it is surprising how many adults believe in angels...

Do not drive faster than your angel can fly.

There is a creative and saving possibility in every situation.
  Paul Tillich

Don't be afraid to take big steps.
You can't cross a chasm in two small steps.
  David Lloyd George

We would often be sorry if our wishes were granted.
  Aesop

The house of my being was not secure against the elements.
  Jim Cotter

The UN is not there to bring heaven to mankind
but to save it from hell.
  Dag Hammarskjold (UN Secretary General)

A river can only flow if it has banks,
otherwise the water disappears into swampiness.
So the human being needs boundaries in order to flow,
otherwise it disappears into ineffectiveness.

Face the sunshine and the shadows fall behind you.
  Helen Keller

Conceal your wants from those who cannot help you.
  seen in Bucklers Hard Museum

Share your weaknesses
and you will discover each other's strengths.
   Anon

Only God is perfect so that lets us off the hook. (Q)

It's no good living your life on: What if......?

Death

It is usually assumed we are afraid of death. Why ? There is a
right time for all things and letting go is a necessary part of life.

I owe so large a debt to life,
I feel if I should die today
My death could never quite repay
For friends and mirth and careless laughter.
    Winifred Holtby

When the evening of life comes,
we shall be judged on love.
    St. John of the Cross

Sometimes it seems to me that the only thing we really know
about death is that it is creative.
    Elizabeth Goudge

Death is God's greatest gift to the living.
    Anon

Look upon the dead as your particular friends.
    St Columba

'I shall have to put my skates on.'
'Why ?'
'Because I must put my house in order and
 I may not have long to go....'. (much laughter). (Q)

Worship and Praise

Regular worship perpetually renews our sense of hope and belonging.
Without a sense of praise, life feels flat.

The test of good worship is the love it creates.
  Anon

Some people's heart is too hurt to praise
but one can praise with one's intent. (**Q**)

In the prison of his days. Teach the free man how to praise.
  W. H. Auden

And all the windows of my heart I open to the day.
  John Greenleaf Whittier. (**Q**)

Who would have thought my shrivelled heart
Could have recovered greenness ?
  George Herbert

Two builders, when asked what they were doing,
The one replied: I lay bricks.
The other: I'm helping to build a Cathedral.

The highest form of worship is service to man.
  quoted by Andrew Carnegie

Let us praise our Maker, With true passion extol him.
  W. H. Auden

Without worship we think we have to live life in our own strength,
and we try ever harder, and get worn out – or disillusioned.
Only within worship does the understanding of grace
come that perpetually revivifies. (Q)

It's a poor heart that never rejoices.
   A proverb

At the summit of Everest, to mark the occasion, Tensing left chocolates
and sweets for the gods; Hilary left John Hunt's cross beside them.

Purpose, religion, commitment

The quote I like best out of all these is Rose Macaulay's :
'Once you get into the area of religion, everything is a bit odd.' Religion
engages our deepest emotions and for that reason is the most difficult to
pin down. For most people it suggests purpose and meaning in life and it
expects commitment.

A child said of flowers: Why paint them ? They are already there.

A small child asked: Why are we here on earth, Mummy ?
Mother answers: To help others.
Small child: Why are the others here?

It is one of life's duties to cheer people up with witticisms.
   Eileen Yeoman

His heart is in the right place, he's just going a different route.
   Anon

Guard for me my feet upon the earth....
lest they be bent on profitless errands.
   Early Irish

Most people see my music as being on the sunny side.
Maybe I was put into the world to cheer people up.
   John Rutter

The function of religion is to lift the load.
   Anon

Religion is not assent to some good ideas.
It is commitment to a way of life.
   Anon

The Celts preferred to see questions as mysteries to be lived rather than problems to be solved.

The fanatical atheists and the religious fanatics are creatures who cannot hear the music of the spheres.
Albert Einstein

I sought my soul but my soul I could not see.
I sought my God but he eluded me.
I sought my brother and found all three.
Anon

If religion is any good at all it is inside you.
Otherwise it's just clothes.
Iranian engineer

Once you get into the area of religion everything is a bit odd.
Rose Macaulay

We are all humble learners in the school of Christ.
Edgar G. Dunstan (Q)

A lot of faith is acceptance (Q)

Know all the theories,
Master all the techniques.
But as you touch a human soul
Be just another human soul.
Carl Jung

True godliness don't turn men out of the world but enables them to live better within it and excites their endeavours to mend it.
William Penn (Q)

God calls us not to be successful but to be faithful.

I pin my hopes to quiet processes and small circles in which vital and transforming events take place.
   Rufus Jones (Q)

You can be committed to finding out. (Q)

To know that you are upheld before the Lord is the greatest blessing (Q)

There is a destiny that makes us brothers,
None takes his way alone.
All that we send into the lives of others
Comes back into our own.
   Anon

Prayer

Prayer is a much more natural activity than one might suppose...

When I pray, a power comes to meet me,
across the frontier of my own fear.
    Lionel Blue

Please, thank you, sorry – the words of humility.

The ability to pray is a gift.
    Anon

God – to a man saying his prayers:
For heaven's sake go to bed and let me do the worrying.
    Norman Vincent Peale (Chaplain to the White House)

May your God go with you.
    Dave Allen

Prayer is caring with heart and mind. (**Q**)

Yes, no, wait.
God is not a Father Christmas or a slot machine. (**Q**)

'You know me.
I don't believe but say one for me.'
    In conversation

To discover prayer is to discover a new dimension of human living, a
gate-way out of the high-wall garden of this world's concerns, into the
open country of the love of God.
    Anon

Keep praying, but be thankful that God's answers
are wiser than your prayers.
    Anon
A non-believer to his wife who'd gone to Mass :
"There she goes, God-bothering again."

He prayeth best who loveth best
All things both great and small.
    Samuel Taylor Coleridge – The Ancient Mariner

The papers can be one's prayer-book. (**Q**)

Prayer is the effort to live within the spirit of the whole.
    Samuel Taylor Coleridge

Prayer is like watching for the kingfisher.
All you can do is be where he is likely to appear, and wait.
    Ann Lewin

Prayer is an exercise of the spirit as thought is of the mind.

Study is a kind of prayer.
    Karen Armstrong

Prayer is engagement with life. (**Q**)

When in doubt, I talk to God, and find my mind relieved,
and a way suggested.
    Abraham Lincoln

Prayer is the soul's sincere desire
Uttered or unexpressed.
    James Montgomery

The Bible

For some reason I have always loved the Bible but it is a very misunderstood book. I hope these sayings open up a different way of looking at it and the significance of its central character, Jesus.

I sometimes wonder which Bible people are reading
when they tell me religion and politics don't mix.
Archbishop Desmond Tutu

The Bible is alive, it speaks to me;
it has feet, it runs after me;
it has hands, it lays hold of me.
Martin Luther

This enigmatic figure who came out of Galilee.
Albert Schweitzer

The truth is, the Galilean has been too great for our small hearts.
H. G. Wells

The Bible is to be read not as dogma but as literature
in some sense inspired, not as a science but as poetry.
Matthew Arnold (1822–88)

Your word is a lamp to my feet and a light to my path.
Psalm 119: 105

Celtic spirituality says all you need is
nature on the one hand and the Bible on the other.

A hundred years from my death the Bible will be a museum piece.
Voltaire (1694 – 1778)

The Revelation of God is not a book or a doctrine but a living Person.
  Emil Drummer

Love

*Love is the essence of life. It is many-sided and with
varying levels of depth, demands and even humour.*

Self drives; love draws. (**Q**)

He that plants trees, loves others beside himself.
  Thomas Fuller – 1732

'My husband has courted me all my life.'
  Anon

On a poster:
Love your enemies.
It will drive them nuts.

All human beings are loveable, sociable and non-violent.
  *Bob Johnson (**Q**) – James Naylor Foundation*

If someone loves you enough you're real.
  Margery Williams in The Velveteen Rabbit.

'I know God loves me. He has to. He's God.
But does he like me?' (**Q**)

You can learn to love your duty. (**Q**)

In Western society we need affection with sexuality.

Unto him who is everywhere we come by love
and not by navigation.
  St. Augustine

The real question is not what you have done but how lovingly
you have done it; how you have manifested love in your life.
   David Lorrimer

We can do no great things; only small things with great love.
   Mother Teresa

Love is the hardest lesson in Christianity;
but for that reason, it should be most our care to learn it.
   William Penn. (Q)

Thou art but a little thing, yet he loveth thee,
and holdeth thee in the hollow of his hand.
   Julian of Norwich

Forgiveness

Forgiveness is the other side of love. Sometimes we need to
forgive life for what it does to us – even forgive God...

You are able to forgive when you no longer
feel you have to improve the past.
    Anon

God forgives sins, otherwise heaven would be empty.
    – seen on a poster (and God would be lonely...! (Q))

Out of the crooked timber of humanity
no straight thing can ever be made.
    Immanuel Kant

To err is human; to forgive divine.
    Alexander Pope

To err is human, to persist in error is devilish.
    St Augustine of Hippo

To withhold forgiveness from another feeds a sense of power
because I can give forgiveness or not. (Q)

He who forgives ends the quarrel.
    African proverb.

Forgiveness is not an occasional act, it is a permanent attitude.
    Martin Luther King

Your guilt is not helping you.
Your penance is to love.
    R4 service from St Martin in the Fields

The African heart says: If a person is truly sorry for what they have done,
the one who is wronged will try and find it in their heart to forgive.

In ancient shadows and twilights
Where childhood had strayed,
The world's great sorrows were born
And its heroes were made.
In the lost boyhood of Judas
Christ was betrayed.
  George William Russell

Hugo Gryn, Chief Rabbi, when asked
if he could forgive Auschwitz, said:
There are some things only God can forgive.

One can forgive life being harsh if people are kind (Q)

The Orthodox Churches begin Lent with Forgiveness Sunday.

Mozart's music always makes me feel forgiven.
  Anon – heard on R4

Cost of life

I have always understood that any great good in life has a cost.
A musician, say, or sportsman, must give up much normal childhood
activities to reach the top. Parents sacrifice much for their children. And
within life there is bound to be an element of suffering.

Certain things cannot be seen except by eyes that have wept.
   Louis Venillot.

Jesus did not say:
You shall not be tempted
you shall not be travailed
you shall not be afflicted
but he said:
you shall not be overcome.
   Julian of Norwich

A ceaseless sowing; an unknown reaping.
   Anon

You have the privilege of knowing those who suffer.
Do not step aside from that path. (Q)

Life is not a matter of playing a good hand
but of playing a poor hand well.

Give your blood and God will give you his Spirit.
   The Ancient Fathers

We can only appreciate the miracle of the sunrise
if we have waited in the darkness.
   Anon

I see God as the wound and not the bandage.
Dennis Potter – in his last interview

It changes your expectations and outlook on life,
having a handicapped child.
A parent

There is a creative and saving possibility in every situation.
Paul Tillich

If you are committed, you will find the magic. (**Q**)

Worry dies not rob tomorrow of its sorrow
but it does rob today of its strength.
Concentration camp victim

'Strange blossoms spring from the anguish of life' ten years after
the tragedy of Dunblane –
quoted from Auden

For those who have suffered, the way to God is by healing and abundance; for those who have always had everything and been successful in life, maybe the way to God is through self-sacrifice. (**Q**)

You accept the sacrifice. (**Q**)

"Almighty" means there is no situation
out of which good cannot be brought.
Anon

Suffering, while it often degrades,
can sometimes ennoble.
Lord Longford

Adversity is the diamond dust heaven polishes its jewels with.

Anon

Your neighbour is the altar on which you
make an offering of yourself to God.

Anon

Belief

Belief is an elusive quality. For some it is an absolute necessity;
for others it raises unanswerable questions and is always
shadowed by its opposite, doubt.

If the sun and moon should doubt,
They'd immediately go out.
    William Blake

When men stop believing in God,
they don't believe in nothing;
they believe in anything.
    G. K. Chesterton

Think of God as a working hypothesis. (**Q**)

Faith is not so much an intellectual belief in the existence of God,
as an attitude of heart and mind that says: there must be an answer
to this somehow. (**Q**)

Faith is greater than belief. Embrace uncertainty.
    Anon

Belief develops with life experiences. (**Q**)

Belief is what you have committed yourself to.(**Q**)

I believe in the sun even when it is not shining.
I believe in love even when I feel it not.
I believe in God even when he seems to be silent.
    Written by a Jew in WW2 on the walls of his cell.

I believe that God is in me as the sun is in the colour and fragrance
of a flower – the Light in my darkness, the Voice in my silence.
  Helen Keller

A miracle is an event that creates faith. Frauds deceive. An event that
creates faith does not deceive. Therefore it is not a fraud but a miracle.
  G. B. Shaw

We had the experience but missed the meaning.
  T. S. Eliot

Some people need a simple faith. (Q)

'the junk and treasure of our ancient creeds.'
  Anne Ridler – poet

We all play our part. Only God plays the crucial role.
  Anon

Oh, let us never, never doubt
What nobody is sure about!
  Hilaire Belloc

That's faith, isn't it. If the alternative is despair,
faith is a better option. (Q)

We need to belong before we can believe. (Q)

Brian Redhead: Like many intelligent men, he had a ragbag of convic-
tions which satisfied him intellectually and spiritually but which, when
you put them together, could not be readily labelled.

Faith must be reinforced by reason. Faith without reason is blind.
  Gandhi

'I sometimes think I'd like to be an atheist
but God doesn't let me.'
   In conversation

Believe in spite of the evidence and see the evidence change.

At the heart of the world's major religions lies the shared belief that
compassion is the key to spiritual awareness.
   Karen Armstrong

God and Humanity

My humanity is the road by which I must travel.
Suso

God moves anonymously on the inside of life.
Martin Buber

In God we live and move and have our being.
St. Paul

Jesus is as much of God as can be contained in human form.
Anon

True godliness don't turn men out of the world but enables them to live better in it and excites their endeavours to mend it.
William Penn. (Q) 1682

God does not die on the day we cease to believe in a personal deity, but we die on the day when our lives cease to be illumined by the steady radiance, renewed daily, of a wonder the source of which is beyond reason.
Dag Hammarskjold – UN Secretary-General

George Fox urged Friends to 'take care of God's glory.'